M000306104

SACRED CONVERSATIONS

PREVIOUS COLLECTIONS

The Company of Strangers (1975)
The Room Where Summer Ends (1979)
Nightseasons (1983)
The Van Gogh Notebook (1987)
The Astonished Hours (1992)

SACRED
CONVERSATIONS

Poems by Peter Cooley

Carnegie Mellon University Press
Pittsburgh 1998

ACKNOWLEDGMENTS

Grateful acknowledgment is made to the editors of the following magazines in which these poems, or versions of these poems, first appeared:

The Big Easy, Crescent City that Care Forgot: "Poem for the Moment of My Death"
Borderlands: "A Vision"
Crab Orchard Review: "To My Son on His Eleventh Birthday"
Crazy Horse: "The Return," "At the Special Olympics," "The Crow"
Defined Providence: "Little Mad Song"
Denver Quarterly: "Why I Despise Myself"
Doubletake: "I Have to Tell You This"
Indiana Review: "Dusk," "No Land of Counterpane," "Poem on My Birthday"
The Iowa Review: "To Emily Dickinson in New Orleans," "Morning After My Death"
Kenyon Review: "Incantation"
New England Review: "Rites of Passage," "The Sea Birds"
North Atlantic Review: "For Gregor Samsa"
The Ohio Review: "Eventides"
Poetry: "Poem on the First Day of School," "Messengers," "Psalm Before Sleep,"
    "Transcendentals," "Poem on the First Day of Spring," "Vespers"
Poetry International: "For Hamlet," "In Possibility"
Poetry Northwest: "Monuments," "To My Hypocrite Reader"
Prairie Schooner: "To The Reader," "To the Sun," "For Daisy Miller," "Museum
    Piece," "Driving, Christmas Eve"
Shenandoah: "For Tess of the d'Urbervilles"
Shimer Roundtable: "No Moral Lesson," "November, Another Poem on My Birthday"
Southern Poetry Review: "Coincidental Music," "Sources"
The Southern Review: "For Lear," "Body of Night," "For Jay
    Gatsby,"
Virginia Quarterly Review: "Hunger," "Against Imagining"
Willow Springs: "For Arthur Dimsdale"

Publication of this book is supported by a grant from the Pennsylvania Council on the Arts.

Library of Congress Catalog Card Number: 97-65563
ISBN 0-88748-255-4
ISBN 0-88748-256-2 Pbk.
Copyright © 1998 by Peter Cooley
All rights reserved.
Printed and bound in the United States of America.

10 9 8 7 6 5 4 3 2 1

"Museum Piece" appeared in *Grow Old Along With Me* (Papier Maché Press)
"A Vision" appeared in *The Sacred Place,* edited by W. Scott Olsen and Scott
Cairns (University of Utah Press)
"Poem on the First Day of Spring," "Morning After My Death," "For Tess of
the d'Urbervilles" appeared in *1995/1996 Anthology of Magazine Verse and
Yearbook of American Poetry* (Monitor Book Company)

I wish to thank Sandra Haro without whose help this book would not have
been possible.

To my wife, my children and my parents

CONTENTS

I

To My Hypocrite Reader   13
To the Sun   15
For Tess of the d'Urbervilles   16
The Return   17
Dusk   20
Poem for the Moment of My Death   21
Hunger   22
For Lear   24
My Raven   26
Against Imagining   27
For Jay Gatsby   28

II

Monuments   33
For Daisy Miller   34
Rites of Passage   35
A Vision   36
Museum Piece   37
For Anna Karenina   38
Holy Hour   40
Postprandial: The Landings, A Retirement Center
    Offering an Independent Lifestyle   41
Morning After My Death   42
No Moral Lesson   43
In Place of Happiness   44
The National Cremation Society   46
I Have to Tell You This   47

III

Attempt at Elegy   51
No Land of Counterpane   53
Poem on the First Day of School   54
Transcendentals   55
The Video Arcade   56
To Emily Dickinson in New Orleans   58
Coincidental Music   59
For Jake Barnes   60
At the Special Olympics   62
For Hamlet   63
The Sea Birds   65

IV

Messengers   69
In Possibility   70
Poem on My Birthday   71
For Arthur Dimsdale   72
Brother Body   73
For Jude the Obscure   75
Body of Night   77
Why I Despise Myself   78
To My Son on His Eleventh Birthday   79
Little Mad Song   80
For Ozma of Oz   81
Sources   83

V

For Emma Bovary in Heaven   87
November: Another Poem on My Birthday   89
The Crow   90
Driving, Christmas Eve   91
Psalm Before Sleep   92
Incantation   93
For Gregor Samsa   94
Vespers   95
To the Reader   96
Eventides   97
Poem on the First Day of Spring   98
Invitation to the Voyage   99

All the world exists
to end in a book.

—Mallarmé

1

So we beat on, boats against the current,
borne back ceaselessly into the past.

—F. Scott Fitzgerald, *The Great Gatsby*

TO MY HYPOCRITE READER

Every day in motion, these wheels under me,
the city swarming around me, every season
another summer surrounding my glassed-in world,
this cool sarcophagus urging me on.
And at the edge of my eyes, the multitudes,
the poor always with us, wandering the roadsides,
those who beg at intersections or forage uncut grass
for a bottle, a tin can, to sell back at dinner time.

Reader, come with me, guide my hand,
I need directions, turning. I need
to keep my words steady going down.

New Orleans, unreal city . . . I have nowhere to be
myself, no room can bear my body's hunger
for taking down the shadows, the armatures of all I see:
the three-legged dog in heat on the church steps;
the whores letting down straps of pastel sundresses,
tanning their breasts across the balcony of their motel.
Yawning, they wave to me, always plying their trade.

And now, street after street of houses abandoned
to those with no house, windows knocked out.
Nausea: the wheels spin me on.

Reader, without you, I have no one.
This sickness quickens me. I feed on it.
I am thrilled by my own illness. Be my friend.

Vertigo: the wheels spin me on:
crows, gulls, bent over patches of black water
between cracks in the road; a pelican,
lost inland, wanders, one leg broken, a used car lot,
flapping and stumbling, passed over by a man
of the cloth, white collar riding a rusted motorbike,
a sign on his chest, another on his back,
HAVE YOU BEEN WASHED IN THE BLOOD OF THE LAMB?

Reader, drive for me. I have nothing
here to hold me as, rung by rung,
I go down the old ladder of terror
attaching itself to a stone wall, shaking
the foundations of despair which may,
any step, give out as I straddle the blind air,
rising at morning to wander, to pass the day in transit
out-of-doors, feeding on this city, its liver, heart and brain,
no other way to satiate this need to leave myself.

TO THE SUN

Whatsoever things your light comes to today
will be beyond my choosing. This is what I love
about the moment just before you rise,
why I am up, coffee in my hand, ready to toast
the oaks in the backyard, the shrouds they took at midnight
you will strip from them that they begin their morning naked.
Oh, everything else is work in the business of the world,
love most of all, the body rushing to it, the mind
hungry, too, for its own kind or an explanation,
the heart, that intercessor, will accept on faith . . . .
Enough. Here in this gulf city, the cloud cover
by noon will put out my vision of you, probably,
and I'll be in one of the usual funks, stalled
at the side of my own road, while you stride on,
dividing heaven, thinking I don't know what
of those who walk beside you, risen from me.

FOR TESS OF THE D'URBERVILLES

Such abundance of summer, the tremulous
suspension of our terror, knowing we will die
coming out to meet the morning at our feet,
a ripe light never witnessed until this minute.
All things, the ants' percussion on the sidewalk,
the mourning doves' accompaniment, the sun at noon
beginning its ascent now among the chorus of the oaks,
all are caught up, rising, in our singing, ceaseless.
This is the morning you went out to, Tess,
believing in the prospects of the field at dawn
which had no end in sight if you could trust
the sky enough to cup you in its hands.
Few now would hold to this—although I do—
the immortals have their daily sport with us,
loosing the web on mornings we run toward
so we believe we have eluded the doom mark
even as we see it laid out on our palm
or moving toward us evenings on the lawn,
assuming the tentacles of shadows, crawling upward.
Even I, who have been married twice,
once to this wife but first and always my whole life
to darkness, the first skin I slipped inside,
I, too, revel in the ecstasy of this deception—
summer is immortal it tells us, in the flowering vine,
the blue stare of the hydrangeas mirroring the sky
so we must be, as we rush out to it, we think,
mirrors, too, and not the flies the gods have made us,
our black voices fitted to windows of the immortals,
swarming there until one by one we drop.

THE RETURN

A bird in the house means death,
my grandmother always said,
death is back, but I never saw it

the ten years she lived with us
though death's invisible claws
or something more than a wren's

extend themselves from the body
I'm chasing over my house tonight.
Thank God my wife's asleep—

she'd insist it's a bat,
that the children should be spirited
to a motel. The wren dazzles me:

I could be staggering a savannah of heat
the middle of Africa and ahead a butterfly
hobgoblining these lampshades' white linens:

here the teak lamp, there the speckled pyramid,
now the bookcase, the tobacco jar
Grandma left me, swearing I'd smoke later.

All the men in our family have it in their blood,
another maxim like *Red Sky in the Morning,*
Sailor Take Warning, Red Sky

at Night, Sailor's Delight,
she warbled my whole childhood
before she was a child at the dinner table

every five minutes or so demanding
of my mother, *What time is it?* and of my father
Do you remember when I was a little girl how . . .

Then once I spit my water out, gut-busting
when she called me Father and my father
banished me to my room where I cursed her

to my friend on the phone, my voice cracking,
hooting over the loony, planning an evening
with the girl just one of us would dare to call.

Now the bird tiptoes the lid
of the tobacco jar and lifts it,
unearthing my pipe tobacco's rank scent

and I remember my grandmother
filled the jar with paper clips
toward the end and cracked them open

each morning in a necklace
she took apart hour by hour until she slept.
The bird is pure intelligence,

I think, entering the hall
where it precedes me, fluttering,
in one of the side rooms like my bedroom

Grandma ceased to notice
as her cataracts clouded and that door ajar
in my parents' house sent her tumbling

till she went down, spinning,
her hip never stitching the bones back together
so she could leave the hospital and live with us again.

Already I had left for college and forgotten
even water-spitting when Father phoned:
the last hour she repeatedly had called my name.

So guilt it is I'm chasing through rooms tonight,
this creature I need to get outside
in the night air, to pose some questions to:

suppose you are who I think you are?
Is it too early or too late to ask
how will it be when I come back myself,

my voice, diminuendo, strung out on some branch,
tiny as the body of this soul?
Will you give me even the flutter

of an answer if I catch you in my palms?
Your warm feathers throbbing the prow of my lifelines
till I release you to the night sky before it's light?

DUSK

You know this hour between the hours.
In summer it draws down the night to you.
It stands on edge above your head, it stares
back at you from nowhere, promising everything.
Now the hunchbacked tailor and his seamstress
behind the steam presser undo each other's buttons;
now the mouths of the peonies quiver to close
over the last bees plunging together, deeper.
And the three-legged dog, wobbling, claims his bride.
This is the hour the suicides change their minds
and decide to peroxide their bangs or go bowling;
when nuns masturbate while the spider kneels to the west
where you are looking out at what will not come right
tomorrow again, rising, and count its sinking sweet
and go out to find a place beside someone in the oblivion.

POEM FOR THE MOMENT OF MY DEATH

Today again I saw you, brother, you are the Fat Man
navigating his exit from the bus at eight a.m.
where South Carrollton intersects, defying physics,
whimsy, logic, semantics, grammar,
South Claiborne so the gutters flood New Orleans
each time it rains and yesterday you turned to me,
stalled at the stoplight. You were fat with rain,
drenched with the waters which preceded us,
all things man-sown, born of women, you were fat
with a hunger to murder anyone drinking the rain
or abstaining as I was while the waters of the sky
protected me from the stiff bulge in your pants,
the gun you fondle like another member,
one you have not lost to the spoils of your waist.
That was yesterday. Today is clear. You look right through me.

HUNGER

I

Nearer to heaven, though she disclaims its presence,
my mother, since I last saw my parents,
a visit to them confirms, naps longer
each afternoon, awakening to prepare dinner,
always a great event for her, the readying of others' pleasure.
Even if my father and I are not hungry
we have long learned to fake a ravenous appetite
for her latest Salade Niçoise or Poulet Orange
or whatever these cookbooks from around the world serve up.
She eats slivers, brags she weighs two pounds more
than at her wedding sixty years back.
Dad waxes proud, head nodding, false teeth orchestrating
his best efforts on a chunk of filet doused in burgundy.
Like all of us, I am a child again, going home
where I hear the old adage in my head, sitting down now:
Pretend you're eating with the queen and king; eat slowly.
As a child, I hated it. Now I see cutting everything up fine
to eat with mincing bites just piquancy
to love longstanding, theirs for each other,
ours. I think I'll go for seconds in a minute
on the Bavarian Chocolate Cake. Tomorrow my wife
will help me start my diet. I'll have to ask her,
however, since she doesn't talk with food
about affection, only with words.

II

My time has come to go, I can't sleep,
my aunt, ninety-two, announces to me
long distance, as if I knew the window
she will fly through, even though
her body, aching from arthritis,
is in as good a working order as my own
at fifty. Her sentence hangs over the miles between us
until I open my hands to release the feeble bird
squawking, *Oh, you don't mean that,* devouring her words
as if he could grow fat on the silence I consign her to.
Putting down the phone now that she says she must go,
I wonder how the soul, so ravenous, year after year,
can come to have enough of earth after awhile
that hunger and thirst are slaked entirely.
If only she believed in heaven, if I could make her,
I would know where she conceived herself to be
when this is over, though I can put her there
later whenever I want, but still wish she had one of her own,
a blue vault she could pray to, a little infinite
limited just for her, so she could sleep at night.

FOR LEAR

I have to get this down before the light dies.
That leaves me thirteen minutes before sunset at 6:14.

A minute gone already? Here I go, the best I can:
my mother called at dawn; my father's in the hospital

again, reason unknown, and I saw my own exhaustion,
half a century's staggering toward me at noon

crazed, so the afternoon, out of time,
was a kind of night, starless, cloudless, sleepless,

where I wandered, terrified and cold
though the gulf wind bearing me along New Orleans' streets

tried to tell me the end will be a kind of balm
such as the drowned know, surrendering their bodies.

I have to say this: every year now
you are increasing in my life, Lear.

I see you in the old man living in the parking lot
of my bank, sleeping on moneybags emptied

of the world's currencies, and the tellers appear
punching in to give him table scraps for his repasts

while the cops and street gangs hail him and pass on.
Or the other ancient one, shopping cart his home,

who wanders the highway, preaching to passing traffic,
or the legless one who begs cathedral steps all day.

These have all survived themselves. Who am I to know
if my father—if I—will be passed over

as these have been when the reaper swings through,
determined to curb the excess of our numbers, Lear,

as if some should be spared to parade a fine madness
such as I hope to display in motley, growing old

but would not wish on my father in his mildness,
and as I, too, might imitate against my inclination

when the button will not be undone, when my time comes.

MY RAVEN

Once, when I was in the spirit,
without asking, the house still, my wife asleep,
the raven came, the one you all know about.
What it quoted to Poe it repeated back to me
so I knew even when he professed he wrote that poem
according to the rules in his "Philosophy,"
the essay I never believed in, he had based it on this single word
which has endured and will endure through time eternal.
I had no bust of Pallas, but it perched
above the doorway, anyway, in my study
and, when I put the question to it, said
one vision in a lifetime was enough for me.
To those greater, greater would be given, maybe,
but I must make do with single vision or else none.
Since then, I've tried otherwise. How have I done?

AGAINST IMAGINING

Onomatopoeia he would tell you
if he knew the word, this skittering report
of his arms against the wheelchair's wheels,
the screeching unbroken. I always catch him,
my next-door neighbor in his promenade
down and up our street which is his world
since the stroke. And now, as I speak, he's back
to his chairlift depositing the apparatus
on that front porch where he will watch all afternoon
as if stargazing might turn the day to night.

I don't want to mythologize. And yet
his concentration on the sky itself,
so unutterably blue, absolutely
cloudless all summer, which I've tried to hold
within my eyes, I can't put out of mind.
Once he was a gambler who had to drive a cab
even in New Orleans, he told me, as a cover.
Now he wheels and deals the infinite
which has been forced by necessity to come to him.
You think I made this all up? Just a minute ago
he gave me the materials in his broken speech.
It's for a poem, he said. *I've never read one.*

FOR JAY GATSBY

Once it was the pulse of the green light
where Daisy throbs on and off

at the end of the dock, her promise
the new world stretched out before us—

yes, I believed in that and more than Nick
longed to be your sidekick at parties in the blue dark,

in love with myself and my reflections
inventing a story of myself each step,

the moonlight transfiguring our faces, uplifted,
assuring both of us we would keep this going forever,

no moment ever the same myth.
Now that young man is dead as you are,

face down in the pool's black shallows.
Now it's the scene with the shirts I love

and re-live whenever I need a small bright place
charged, no matter how false, with expectation.

Each time I come here Daisy is weeping, fingering
their pastel splendors: alone with herself

in Gatsby's dressing room, beside the lover
who dressed himself in the most essential of disguises

that he come upon no one he could recognize himself,
no matter what vision he follow of that man: lavender,

apple-green, orange, coral, the palette of jungle birds
too gorgeous to be killed for meat or feather—

these, the gods we turn to without question,
assuring us the beauties of the world are all there is,

and the divine human and survives in metaphor.

II

In this way he lived, not knowing or seeing any possibility of knowing what he was or why he lived in the world, and he suffered so much from that ignorance that he was afraid he might commit suicide, while at the same time he was firmly cutting his own particular path through life.

—Tolstoy, *Anna Karenina*

MONUMENTS

Now, in my car, I am come to one
of the sacred places: it is this tiny,
the moment in time beside my son,
nine years old this morning, riding beside me,
his day at camp minutes away. For now,
there is the music of his voice, off-key
accompanying my own to the car radio
blaring country-and-western. How soon I see
on the wind which carries this music and this car,
this season, this city, this country, this planet,
he will begin to leave me as my parents,
aging quickly now, are leaving me this summer
faster and faster. Moving, I say, I see it on the air.
All things in their permanence are still, written here.

FOR DAISY MILLER

You had to die. It follows naturally
from being original, female, American

right up to the penultimate page, embracing
the night air of the Colosseum in your lungs

you dare to ingest under moonlight with an Italian.
It courses through your blood; you hemorrhage on flirtation.

When I was the age at which you always leave us,
nineteen, I wanted my way in all things, too,

and on a dare drove through the tunnel to Windsor
from Detroit, dead drunk, changing countries and back,

never getting stopped, and now, thirty years later,
would do it again, but only if you dared me.

Thirty years. I have survived myself
and cannot touch my flesh to your flesh across death

no matter how unblushingly the pages undo your sex.
Each time I turn to you, here in moonlight,

I want to know, my hands shaking to embrace the book,
did you sleep with him, the Italian?

You won't tell me, will you? And I have no way to make you,
Daisy, neither father, lover nor author of you.

RITES OF PASSAGE

It wasn't a question of the traffic
though it was Friday and five-thirty,
the hour most of us consider ourselves free.
The cars backed up, stacked up
ahead of me, at either side,
the rainbow of them so muted and pastel
they could have been a vision of the underworld
we would find at the sea's floor if we had eyes to light it.
And maybe they were to the bird in his swoops
earlier when the seascape scrim of clouds nearby
was his habitation. But now the pelican, wings shattered,
flapped from hood to hood,
windshield to windshield, as stupid and bedimmed
as any of us who had seen something in him
when he held up the sky, rising from the sea,
something not for us between his jaws.
I knew he would not survive our journey home
this evening, the journey all of us assumed
would end in our dark pleasures, some of which were innocent.
But when he came to me and my windshield filled with blood
I felt I had been the one to draw him down
so that something like the firmament had visited,
scattering its feathers over which his red profusion
was some necessary consequence. And then, just when
the bumpers unlocked, a crowd of boys swarmed up
out of nowhere, boys too young yet to chase girls,
and they fell on him with sticks, they beat each other,
they divided him up with necks of bottles, pocket knives.
I think they each received a piece of his kingdom
death gave them as a presentiment they could take home
provided they took it as booty, nothing more.
But how could I know? I am no better.
I rushed right back to spill the blood on paper here.

A VISION

I look out at the flowers in the yard.
As if by lightning they have been delivered from their bodies,
crushed and black from last night's frost.
My summer garden: such labor, such tenderness,
fell to the preparation of the soil, the seeds,
rising or not, then the sprouts, lush on the warming air,
before the gashes of color when they were blossoming.
My delphiniums, no, my red-tongued salvia,
I suppose I will miss you most among the worshipped
until some of you appear next year. Now the burden of autumn.
Since I awoke, the flowers have been babbling
unceasingly in their new tongues, being dead,
recognizing in me the soul of a brother
in whom death has planted such darkness, such hunger,
he is greedy for their words, even consuming them, glutted.

MUSEUM PIECE

Each dawn for the man a new face
swims up in his shaving mirror.
The eyes stare back, in charge of everything:
the jawbone, the nose, each year more like his father,
both twisted a little to the left, Cubistic,
rearranged by a seventh-grade football accident.
It is all here: the new day glazed
in stubble he will scrape like an engraver
burning the plate with fine lines of his razor
while he creates himself as while he slept
after sex the night before or during his rush
into the woman or late today at his desk,
the sculptor will be at work on him,
pulling the lines at the sides of his eyes wider,
deepening the crevices on both sides of his nose,
crossing the brow with cross-stitching of its trade,
preparing the corpse handsomely, masterfully,
for his rightful position among contemporaries.

FOR ANNA KARENINA

Because like Levin, married to another,
I, too, have loved you whenever we have met,

lusted after you as he did, drawn
in by your half-closed eyes, your small white hands

flashing with brilliants, your face transfixed,
lit by discipline of passion you surrender,

suspecting Vronsky's every glance at other women . . .
because I tell myself, night after night,

I sleep with my wife to enter you,
sliding inside her body like a tomb

through which I try to resurrect your flesh
that rises with me as we come from Paradise

or the Limbo in which the book of your life
flares up in all that had been shadow,

replaying that instant as the train strikes
to consign you, you pray, to oblivion . . . .

Anna, I cannot speak with reason,
I am too far gone, lovesick, rising

as the night falls and I long to take myself
in hand, imagining you, as now my wife

calls me to accompany her to church.
I stall her off, I bring myself down, hard.

Darling, the bells ring now, their six long peals
announce the Sunday evening Mass. I will be late

for your sake, rushing to finish this.
But when the priest, during Prayers of the People,

asks us whom we pray for, Anna,
in the hope of the resurrection, breathless,

I will, before everyone, speak out your name.

HOLY HOUR

When I stood up I was at prayer.
Mass was over, I heard some shuffling feet
behind me, and candles had been snuffed up front
where I had knelt to take in the body and the blood,
to genuflect and process with others to my seat,
to kneel again, rise, mumble and so on.
But all this while I had been with the clown,
madman, prophet, what-have-you, on his bike
weaving in and out of traffic as I drove off to work—
bowler hat, filthy madras jacket, florid purple
four-in-hand, cheroot, and, I swear to God, spats—
his back sporting a placard, blood-red letters dripping down
to herald the coming of the Lord
while he sang, no, belted hallelujahs,
barreling across the intersection against the light.

Without asking, without wanting, Lord,
I have been in the spirit times like this.

POSTPRANDIAL: THE LANDINGS, A RETIREMENT CENTER OFFERING AN INDEPENDENT LIFESTYLE

Later, a cacophony of television syllables
will swell the separate apartments
until each solitude can fall asleep or nod
over pillage and carnage in the world at large.

But now, light falling, all of them finally back—
having made the trek from dining room to numbered room—
wheelchair, cane and walker come to rest,
and that hour the nurse has told me will not pass
without the wailing begins, and wailing fills the rooms.

She is not alone but joined by others here,
my aunt at ninety-two, picking up the phone
to call me. Uncannily, she times her wailing
as if, within my body, she, too, stepped inside the door.

And now my wife stands by, my children disperse,
bickering for their dinner which will be reheated
while I listen a few minutes, wishing I might cry,
spooning up a few words when I can.
There is nothing more to do now. I am all alone,
she cries, they are all alone, wailing.
There is nothing more to do now.
I am saying what can be said. Nothing now.

MORNING AFTER MY DEATH

Before this dawn, as always, one sparrow, one note:
a piccolo, now a flute, and now another
centering the dark on the fence around my house.
My hollow in the bed beside my wife
cannot hear it. Nor my feet which do not strike the floor,
my body no longer groping for robe, slippers,
my curse which is not here against the cold: none
of what she remembers greets the body of the woman I remember
rising, wrapping herself in hesitation just a second.
And why she pauses, suspended that next second
I can only guess. Instead, I can be certain
this is the instant my birds will begin
together to orchestrate the lifting of the sky.
Here is where imagination has to leave us,
and you, wiser than I, reader, living still,
may find such music in a morning of small things
as permits you to see enormities today may come to.
And give you visions only the dead possess
when I try to come back and must rely upon darkness
turning to dawn, that I not speak too loudly my disguises.

NO MORAL LESSON

Imagine a boy at the height of his kite,
our summer almost over at the beach,
learning how tiny the sky is. He is up here,
riding the spread wings' disappearing red,
glancing at beachcombers and bathers in a swarm
seeking their second body in the tides.
Now he is on the run, releasing string
along the spindle, holding always just a little back
as if he hadn't in his fingers grasped
the entire length of summer, how it was
learning to rise as if ascension has no end.
First there was the thrill of climbing air
where seagulls tred, imitating pinions arcing
upward and downward; then, after the crashes
of the frame he had entered but not wholly
and the mastery he chose next, learning to release
those necessary seconds to his string as it met wind,
then he was the thing, nameless, directionless.
It was not a kite and he was not a boy,
just a scarlet rush of motion thinner than flesh
leaving its song to the streamers of the tail.
Weeks passed like this; I said he was a child once,
he had to learn, even as he went on, rising,
nothing we think ours is anything but what we've borrowed.
This is a poem about my son at nine—
all summer he has learned to hate such slack
as perfection knows when we fly out along its course.
No, I am lying. This is not about my son,
though it is true he has a kite I gave him
by which I have been all summer on the wing.
I wanted you to read this about me.

IN PLACE OF HAPPINESS

First my son's name, of course.
She was eighty-three at his birth,
hardly knew it then. Next my younger daughter,
then my oldest, soon to be married,
a fact I announce to my aunt, the hush thickening
which tracked us here as I wheeled her down
to the sunroom where I am doing, against my will,
all the talking except when she says *What?*
Now it is my wife's name she has lost,
now, the next second, my wife she loved
like the daughter she never had when she asks,
Did you ever get married? looking up,
tears between her eyes, not in them,
asking me again *What? What?* Who am I,
I conjecture, or what or why
am I? I am because I am
here, and then, not very funny, wise guy, and then
she cries, *Is my mother still alive?*
There's no more to say. It's getting late
I say to the liver-spotted dots in the linoleum
I've talked to weeks now and then to the magnolia
loosing its white cusps at the window
which has witnessed this day with the room's inhabitants
year on year before either of us arrived here.
I ring for the nurse to take her back,
I give her one kiss she will lose touch with seconds later.
Now, outside on the freeway's give-and-take
of gunning it and braking, sitting on the horn,
I can return to what I prayed for driving over
in expectation of even worse than this:
that soon, one by one, the names appear to her
among the first lights of the village
when it comes in sight and all things return

to their new names, one or legion
as she gives up speaking or being spoken to
in place of happiness, gives up her body, finally
to those waiting there she must pretend
the first few seconds out of time she's never seen before.

THE NATIONAL CREMATION SOCIETY

What will I be, finally, I ask tonight at bedtime,
emptied of the body or the mind?
Because I think flesh does return to earth
in its own fashion, considering those ashes
scattered today by officials of the prim business
facing the highway in this retirement city
where their services are advertised at night in neon
as if burning could be had any hour for a price.
If mind were supposed to return to earth, what might it offer?
The light my own has thrown has been so insubstantial—
witness these poor shadows I have drafted
as if words could for a second hold the touch
of a living hand, imitate in motion cunt and cock
in syncopation. The body dead is more eternal.

I HAVE TO TELL YOU THIS

I wake up and I am in the spirit.
I think: I am dead, but no, I am stretching the same body
I put to bed. My pillow sticks against stubble
from the old drooling habit. But I am in the spirit.
My pajamas cling, they are a second body,
tart with the sour apple smell I know is me.
My wife stirs in her separate continent
inches away, she is fording her own rivers,
breath quickening to the course, but I am in the spirit.
And the light standing at the window now commands
that I not speak. He has been out all night, he says,
walking the water, and it is the voice I recognize
from visits before this. And the hand the light lifts
to assure me the wound there corresponds to mine
is but another certainty the rite has run its course
almost, from which so little will be available
once today is set in motion on the wheel—
God! Always the same, everything lost to it, finally!
I am in the spirit, which I'm leaving just by saying it.

III

It might be lonelier
Without the Loneliness—
I'm so accustomed to my Fate—
Perhaps the Other—Peace—

Would interrupt the Dark—

And crowd the little Room—

—Emily Dickinson

ATTEMPT AT ELEGY

for my Aunt Margaret, 1901-1994

I

You're going to be dead over and over
forever now that you're out of time.
You're going to be out of your body
God knows where in the plains of oblivion,
if there are any, or another habitation
somewhere or nowhere. You're going to be speaking
to me in the voice of the dead
which is my voice claiming I hear yours in it
so all I'm doing is calling myself
trying to come to you. Oh, Aunt, I don't care
that the language of death is nothing we can make up
living. You see, I hear you now:
We all live on borrowed time, you told me as a child,
then threw the ball back across the playroom floor.
I crawled for it. I see us. I'm crawling now.

II

This is how I will remember you.
Not the old lady in the nursing home
who no longer knew my name though she recalled
my face in moments only to lose it
as the summer light, overcast last July,
reflected in syncopation our conversation
of departure: both of us gone already
from each other while we tried to talk.
Here is where I was and am: I'm five,
right by your side as you, amazed,
squeeze my hand to discover I can read,
I've taught myself so we will read together,

I think it was THE POKEY LITTLE PUPPY.
I can hear us now. The book and you and me:
one sound. I go on hearing us as I complete this—
in between, last week, Death stepped in
to say enough to your half of the memory.
And then you turned from me, and gave me up to myself, dying.

NO LAND OF COUNTERPANE

I'm sick because I'm bad like him, I think,
holding up THE TALE OF PETER RABBIT
I've memorized my three months in bed.
This is pneumonia in 1946. It means no appetite
for anything but words. It means I skip the rest of first grade.
From here I date my fascination with the universe
of cannot and will not. Behind drawn shades
I am a body I tear at, that small stalk my center
for grappling and abstinence, satiety, repentance.
And afterwards my hands have no less pleasure
tracing the fables for Peter I throw against the wallpaper
in a sickroom which stages my lamplit finger plays;
all day I march my hero into Mr. McGregor's garden
to replenish the homefront with playmates for a bad boy—
I want more from my namesake than these sisters Potter chose:
Peter Weasel, Peter Badger, all Peter's friends I call Peter!
And yet the father whom McGregor had baked into a pie
is no contender for the measure of his mother's love like mine
whose footsteps on the stairway every night at six o'clock
restore me to the world as he enters with the doctor
and I put away the one I call my own for half an hour.

POEM ON THE FIRST DAY OF SCHOOL

All night the priestesses of wisdom have been practicing
the orders I remember of obedience,
silence and devotion to their measured tones,
index fingers hushed across their lips.
Consequently, it is pointless to inform them, half-asleep
as I appear, arriving with my son,
how tiny I am in my own eyes, giving him up
to their language, a guide through fifth grade.
Now he must learn to mouth it as if it were a tongue
by which the world is formed. And he must take a second one
from such images as boys his age barter among themselves
that his words assume their sounds, therefore his own.
I remember. This is how it's done.
This is how I was given to the world.

TRANSCENDENTALS

How many gods I see on the lawn this morning
just after waking. And all of them are me,
struggling within that light my life permits them
to release such forms as I might pray to.
So the world appears, a history of my failures.
Witness: the solitary jay, lifting the cherry laurel's branch
to a shade of amethyst the sun has dipped him in,
heavenly, saintly. For a whole instant
I see through to a center on my own
where a radiance which is not mine
takes me up. I have these minutes
I can believe, you see. Never more than insufficient.

THE VIDEO ARCADE

Although the "Ladies' Room" sports a name,
and the neighboring door, for men, none,

there are no women here. My son, ten today,
has begged for this trip on his birthday.

Now I give him five bucks, set him free,
the only boy among physically mature males.

But these are not kidnappers or molesters,
they are the suburbs' loneliest masturbators.

Here, mastery can be had for the price of a quarter token.
If you slip one in, you can manage with two Joy Sticks

"Total Carnage," a neat guy on a screen lighting up,
grenade in each fist as he soars over cities,

or, in another, you pay for a nuclear missile
to blast with assured success at an arsenal on the moon.

I see my son has chosen pinball, a relic
of my time, but he'll surrender, hardened enough later

to take his place among men, like this tubby adolescent
who makes the sign of the cross while his rocket

takes off, shooting through galaxies; or the twins
in tandem, about twelve, spurting liquid fire into mermaids

wriggling off a moon slung with thick, black moss.
In a few years my son will be hung up there.

I know. I've done my time, a repeat offender,
in these places before they were rigged by computers

to get you up faster and faster toward visions
of coming, harder, again, harder, again . . . .

Jesus, these visions are rising in my son's eyes,
no, I mean my eyes caught in his. And I'm not playing,

just observing as always, myself in other words,
getting off taking this down, fucking it up, of course.

TO EMILY DICKINSON IN NEW ORLEANS

Of course, you knew you were the first.
Remember? We were in Detroit, the city of my birth,
I was thirteen, just over erecting model cars
and lovesick on myself when I found you after school
in the cool of the library alone. What we touched in each other
I heard in a blizzard of words afterwards all year,
scrawling notebooks full of it until my friends
caught me, taught me: you were an old maid, stuff for girls.
And when the girls assumed your place and I found lines
so lightweight to attract them I couldn't write one down,
you sighed. You said I hadn't been the first for you.

This afternoon you scrawled your note in amethyst
discs of rain dotting my window, your address
in Jackson Square, where it's pouring now, midnight.
The cafés, the horse-drawn carriages, the pastel flower stalls
all stand at attention. The rain lifts, falls. Everything is preparation.
How lonely I would look to anyone but you
in your window of the Pontalba Apartments where you watch,
the same taffeta you pressed for me years back
corseted tight about your waist. And I here, bouquet in hand,
wilted and wet like these wild roses, meet your stare,
forbidden by your immortal soul to come up to you.

COINCIDENTAL MUSIC

The guy in the stall next to mine is masturbating
here between flights where I'm squatting in the men's room
attending to one of the other essential functions
I'd have to hurry through, cramped, at cruising altitude.
Enough of that: I have no claim to the scatological.
What I'm tuned to is his voice, the low, plangent moan
I know is the tip-off to what he's getting down to.
I know, in fact, he's delaying the outcome
of what will leave him wondering how desperation
drove him to take himself in hand among others
in a public place, alone.   I'll bet he's trembling,
thinking I'm next door and might shout to the attendant
or I'm gay or I'll strike the wall between us that minute
the reason he came here appears on his fingers
and he begins to fall into shame and buttoning up.
But I won't and I'm not and I wouldn't.
I'm glad for him he'll be happy some few seconds soon—
happiness-from-grief, oh, I'm grateful just to hear this
as I do now, that I can transport something through the day,
the keening grief we long to spill into women if we can
that they let us burst in them, rest inside them a few minutes,
but if we lack women will make do with our own fists . . . .
This is a minor ecstasy, I've found.   And now he's sighing,
coming to the end, as if that sigh gave us all a reason
we're men, solitary, drained, put back together.

FOR JAKE BARNES

Unimaginable except through you—
to have desire for a woman without lust,

without the stiffening in ourselves boys wake to
that first morning we feel by touch alone

today we will be men and rise to it.
This is a hunger for the other sated

after a body opening below us takes our thrusts
announcing little deaths. And then, if love

precede or follow, the act is stamped in memory
though otherwise returns us to ourselves, alone,

the spasms' aftermath announcing through our calm
that we will live forever, transcendent in the flesh,

those moments that it lasts, countable, expendable.
But your state is like Tantalus', forever

without appetite or thirst, racing in place,
and Lady Brett, who sleeps with all your friends,

your enemies, who lusts most just for you,
remains the soulmate never to be satisfied

as men and women quench each other, separate,
having traded their faces for seconds in the act.

Small wonder in your novel you always leave us
at a lunchtime binge, Brett watching

almost abstemious as you consume desire itself
without a taste for anything: suckling pig, five bottles

of *rioja alta,* starving, glutted, wasted, unsatisfied.

AT THE SPECIAL OLYMPICS

Never could my son yodel, yelp himself hoarse
in his parents' arms, his stare all smiles
like that boy's. Never, hand at his crotch,
could he ogle the judge pinning on his place,
fifth in the swim meet. No,
my son, like me, would peer down on victory,
only a blue ribbon worth his sweat.
Just now, he's ten, itching to get home.
I read it in his tightening fists,
his hush shaking since they lined up to dive,
the timing of their mouths against their eyes' timing
off a split second, that split everything.
Let's go, it's late, your mother wonders
where we are. Of course, she'll never know
any more than I what we have witnessed:
the darkness lifting for the parents of that boy
standing between them, all three together,
an instant they will remember they could let go of him.

FOR HAMLET

All afternoon: the rain, monotonous, my prison bars.
This room, the monotony of my body, spirit up against it,

cells within the cell. How is it once
I had to call to you who daily now appear

wrapped in dark clouds, storming my study's view
upon the backyard, to soliloquize and brood,

utterly unasked for? Now you are here, ranting,
the black sun rising as melancholy locks me up

inside a moment I cannot move beyond.
Hamlet, I am sentenced to you, whom I hoped

after my youth to break out of, to be
as other men, outgrowing your indecisions,

vatic and manic, for the world of business
paved with busyness, reorganized each morning.

Now I am too long melancholy, fifty-three,
to shake off these poles in which I vacillate

unable to take hold, seize, articulate
even my love to three children or a wife

without some swoon or rage or savage quip
which answers to the name of action. I would banish

you to a foreign country under false pretense
did I know I would flee myself

in that self-same breath. Hush, brother,
the rain begins to fall more softly

hearing me confessing this. Now you can sleep.
I'll keep the watch all night if need be for your sake.

We have the ghosts of more than fathers between us, stalking.

THE SEA BIRDS

I saw two black shapes in the rain today
divide the beach between them as they stalked
among the other birds, oblivious to all of us.
I was there to feed my flock, the gulls and terns
I tell myself return daily just for me.
Mine are the wounded, the kind I understand.
One has given up a leg, another the feathers
of his right wing, another has nothing but sockets for her eyes.
They peck at my hands, draw blood. We have our hour together.
But those other birds—they were dipped in black
so no inch of them was anything but obvious:
beak, eye, wing and claw as indifferent to me,
refusing my hand, then turning to the gulf
as they will be all-consuming when they take my body
and cease to be these words as they divide me, piece by piece
to such winds as walk the high tide in oblivion.

IV

"I may do some good before I am dead— be a sort of success as a frightful example of what not to do, and so illustrate a moral story," continued Jude.

— Jude The Obscure

MESSENGERS

You who count yourselves among the melancholiacs,
talking to the invisible, will understand
why I seek to find myself and fail
in citizens considered doomed by most.
Consider the families called the mall rats
inhabiting an abandoned shopping center near the river.
You tell me they sell drugs, they sell themselves?
I think petty thievery is their sustenance.
I know, on faith, a child born last New Year's there,
was delivered by fire maintained in an oil drum
stuffed with Christmas wrappings we trashed at a neighboring dump,
and the harbinger who came forth, trumpeting his birth,
was that Elijah, seven feet, palms uplifted to the sky,
who wanders our highways at all hours, proclaiming, declaiming.
One day it's the world's end, the next the world's beginning.
Do you cross his palms as I do with small change
when he accosts you at the stoplight? You say
the child has disappeared, the prophet's left for Armageddon?
I tell you: I hear him in my prayers tonight, wandering
aisles of the shopping center after dinner,
consumed with the search for a birthday gift for my son,
a pair of boxing gloves, a submachine gun, atomic missiles
guaranteed to raise him to stand alone among men.
I who have these voices, too, and turn to you with them.

IN POSSIBILITY

Even as a little one I know this darkness,
nameless. What I did not know:
it can be taught to speak.
I walk with it as the other boys
run past together, barreling against each other,
oblivious to us in the summer light
I see now in part. I am bound up
in myself. I run here, inside.

Deathless, she comes down to me
in the school library just as I begin
to find my body rising, willfully.
She knows a harder dark,
Dickinson tells me, poem after poem,
the heft of hers stretches, a circumference,
my own may lie in. I promise my allegiance:
if I keep speaking, *From this next breath*
all your possibilities will follow me,
she swears, her mouth over mine,
and no one need ever know our secret.

And then the shadows, together with the light
as they have this afternoon, mid-winter,
possibly may syncopate, and I will walk
transcribing rhythms, stumbling necessarily.
And by such method come to happinesses,
small as they may be, while the years pass through me.

POEM ON MY BIRTHDAY

In the first snowflake imprinting the kitchen window by the sink
my mother, eighty-three, can see the features of the night
I left her for the world. But in this star—
since that is how the prism arranges itself, shimmering—
we are still one body. In an hour from this glimpse
my knocking for release will expel me to the future.
What are we now? She stretches her fingers to her belly,
containing the first kick I will issue from. She remembers:
this is all we are—another night before the window,
summer now and the cicadas beyond the screen
invisible and rasping, drive fissures in the dark
to open for her soul, longing to fly out.
She will not go. She is two souls here
and for awhile she must put off all the world
while I am still inside her. And afterward
wonder the discontent she fed a child
as her own, this man-child never satisfied
while satisfaction, a demon she deliberately puts on,
divides them as she never wished. And so she weeps.
I imagine her tonight especially as she weeps.

FOR ARTHUR DIMSDALE

Last night again I couldn't sleep.
I heard you out there in my yard,
ghostly beside the rosebush where you raise
your scaffold when you pay these visits.
I never asked for this: still, I came out
to stand beside you in my pajamas with the child,
and Hester, and hear your rank confession once again.
Again, I grant such absolution as I can
that you see all four of us gifted with light
meteors dispense these nights we meet in sin,
showering the grace we all believe our privilege.
You tell me each time I have saved you, Arthur,
that without me your soul would shrink and so your body
in the afterlife, that the small penance I assign
allows you to endure your sin I cannot shrive
and so live out your immortality in limbo.
Friend, hear this wherever you walk today,
I only understand you because I have done as much
prison time in sin and escaped just to return,
reveling in my time behind the bars of darkness,
thought, word and deed delicious as I murdered them.
The next night you return why should you not sit down
in my seat at the confessional where you belong?

BROTHER BODY

I

Here I am, awakened by accident
in my motel room, called up by a wrong number
in a sacred place. Brother Body, me,
as St. Francis called his, surrounds the I,
naked the two of us, alone, cold,
this white sheet drawn up by the hands between us
before sleep, halfway home on a long drive,
the business done, here at a dump on the interstate.
If there is happiness, Lord, we can give ourselves,
it is this artless: the gratitude of waking,
my each breath corresponding to the first birds
drawing gold-leaf escutcheons at the window's edges,
the window's centers, the many centers, dark.
Together, You and I will fill them in.

II

This body which was given me to wear
for a little while only, sits here in the diner
no one comes to anymore. It is five o'clock,
the first wash of evening traffic pouring down the street,
car lights strung on the darkening, dividing it.
The ancient waitress, as if preparing me for entrance
into my next life, has baptized me without asking,
calling me "Fred," whenever I stop off for coffee here.
And she blesses bread just by being so negligent
that the roll she brings is always broken.
I am fifty-three. Mornings now my left foot carries such a stiffness

I wonder what route it plans to take with me
in the decade ahead. We will not be together
forever, the flesh and I: when will we be divided?
Should I ask the waitress, priestess of my little rite?

III

Mine, this body I will have to use to die
owning no other while I walk the earth
in anticipation of another walking.
Mine, too, how his ghost answers my stare,
7 a.m., standing before the mirror
wrapped in the shower steam I'm toweling off.
I think the years are gathering around the center
despite whatever push and pull I put it through.
I think I see the landslide I will enter, finally,
has begun its gravitational shift at belly, ass and thighs.
I do not think thinking can hold it back.
Now I'm draping the black towel around my neck,
but I'm no victor staring back at myself, grinning,
my grin a little grave Peter is hiding in.
What fun it will be looking back at this from the hereafter!
I plug in the shaver, lift myself to it. Now today.

FOR JUDE THE OBSCURE

Sometimes I am brought so low
in my melancholy I know only you

can restore me: I turn to your book
in which Hardy has doomed you, line by line.

Taking you down, I have only to touch
the gold-embossed title: now

my transport lifts me as if I had drunk
salvation's cup, eaten its bread.

Then, as I wander the day,
all I pass through are shadows

who would be my wife and children, students
I talk to, spectral, tenebrous,

so consumed am I with guilt
that I must devour you for myself,

take you in as a living sacrifice
who are not Christ but just a man

living only in small print
and then my memory. In his image Hardy made you

to set free someone like myself
from the cage of himself, that, seeing you

I might be for others solace,
respite, or a friend in need,

receiving myself consolation, all of us one
beneath that wheel night and day

turning throughout the sky, imperceptible,
pitiless, rolling over us.

BODY OF NIGHT

If men and women, turning together in sleep
imitate some ancient rhythm
it must be this one, the sea's at night,
the pull and counterpull I am staring into.
The beach is too calm here, the beachwalkers are gone
whose silhouettes in couples I counted on
to hold my eye in place when the light began
leaking westward, trailing gold and pink,
ancient colors irreplaceable with others.
And then it is, despite myself,
everything I have made my whole life,
this hold on nothing as a faith in itself,
that I know all at once the gods are here,
walking the tideline as they did in the old times
to meddle and advise in our affairs—
I see them now, drunk, naked, calling each others' names
as they splash in the sea foam, copulating,
the foam on the sea sprung from them,
the sea and their bodies all one, finally . . . .
Men and women: of course it cannot be like this.
A hundred urgencies of day define whatever body
a man and woman trade, the single tide they swim
multiple and earthly, having nothing of the divine
but mythologies they can recite by rote.
When I go inside, my wife and children will be waiting,
demanding where I was, could we go out to the mall
to buy a new beach ball, to get ice cream, a magazine.
God, I want to go! I need to buy something,
to put a cap on these thoughts before night takes them.

WHY I DESPISE MYSELF

I like to watch happiness.
For the melancholic, staring at its human face
may be all that grace permits.
Witness the couple in the mall you might well laugh at,
reader, unless you, too, traverse this spiral staircase
of shadow and radiance: it is a cage,
but such a one as the tides know, falling, rising,
no moment at their edge ever the same.
But the couple: they were hardly twenty, married,
so fat each limb, and even the appendages, nose, ears,
fingers, swelled with fat, and each wore a baseball cap
on backwards, like every member of the pack of men-boys
roaring at either hand, a prepubescent chorus.
Between them, they swung a little one, two probably,
he, too, so fat you would laugh or weep
to see a child already brought so low.
They were all grinning, they were on their way
to the ice cream store. I want to present this
without irony or scorn or mockery. I want to say,
I mean it, I was restored by them.
I don't know how to say it so you will come with me
into that moment, walking there with happiness.

TO MY SON ON HIS ELEVENTH BIRTHDAY

Once upon a time you were mine entirely.
It was autumn, I was walking home
to your mother, the long way, warmer through the lindens.
The wind stiffened, the trees were watching me
divide the branches, a small path running through them
on which I stagger, fall. When I awake, it is night, starless,
a flock of ravens calling from an upper branch ahead
where the wood divides. As I approach, light glimmers,
a voice among the birds chanting I am chosen
tonight to bear one home to my wife
after which all things miraculous shall happen.
In my hands now the small black clutch of feathers
sings your sweetest, knowing I'll give you up
as the woods thin, your breath coming harder;
soon your mother will appear to take you in
and then your birth begins. Remember, if you can,
who it is extends both hands, palms up,
to release you, claw and beak against his lifeline
into your own life, the one he chose.

LITTLE MAD SONG

You, sky, kneeling down beside the garage tonight
where every root and tuber turns to dust
the instant I look into it, here in your robes
of purple, gold and finally the nakedness
you call darkness and I call my madness,
you, little light, all I have left, pray for me.
There is a night approaching I can't see myself through.

And when I recall those nights I did swim through
to the other side and arrived, revived, only me
rescuing myself, I see the madness
I walk in, stripping to nakedness
as if I could shake my body of the robes
affliction wraps me in, his skin finer than dust.
Sky, hear my prayer, pray all night tonight.

FOR OZMA OF OZ

When I will have descended lower
than this afternoon, even, nothing

to light the day, down in myself
where I have fallen as I write this,

I will stand then, on another afternoon
blacker in early spring, that rain

between me and the green in all things
outside me which is my correspondence,

and touch again the text enchanting myself,
discovering as I did at seven an antidote

to a darkness never lifting in my memory except minutes.
On the last page in which Dorothy says good-bye

forever, decreeing there will be no more books
because in the invisible country she and her friends

depart for, they will not be living, I found myself
a resting place when the world burned too much

in ice or fire, those extremes the polar soul
swings between, and knew by letter

the universe of print, received and welcomed
by Aunt Em and Uncle Henry as if I were their son,

companion of Dorothy as she roamed the volumes,
knowing our home would wait for us in Kansas.

This is the first book by which I found salvation.
After this: every book sacred if I made it.

SOURCES

I have looked too long into the sea tonight.
Like a man who has drunk too much, eaten too much,
I can see nothing but myself when I stare out
and by this I mean the blackness, starless.
Before tonight, I claimed the faces I saw there,
angle on angle, that I might call them Spirit,
or if not that then at least the superhuman
I could tell myself once walked by the Aegean
or the prophet who parted waters for others to believe in
that they might bear witness and choose to follow him.
Too long staring has emptied these same waves
of all things but this I, washing in, washing back,
leaving, as I stand here, stranded at the tideline
the dead still center of the world again.

V

"Whereas the truth is that fullness of soul can
sometimes overflow in utter vapidity of language, for none
of us can ever express the exact measure
of his needs or his thoughts or his sorrows;
and human speech is like a cracked kettle on which we tap
crude rhythms for bears to dance to,
while we long to make music that will melt the stars."

—Flaubert, *Madame Bovary*

FOR EMMA BOVARY IN HEAVEN

He won't let your death stop
but retraces it, step by step

Flaubert loves you so, even in giving you up,
screaming, insisting on your beauty

I can reach out and touch, page 363
where you vomit blood, your pulse

he writes "like a harpstring about to snap."
Emma, sometimes when I go out at night

to walk, I tell myself you have beckoned me
from sleep to find you, spirit,

in the flesh, here near willows by the river
silvered by moonlight, your blouse unbuttoned

still, breathless from your rendezvous
with a new lover in the afterlife

Flaubert has made up just for you.
Years I have dreamed that lover might be me.

Tonight, on the last page of your book again,
I turn to you to take me in,

there where you go on, imagining yourself
with your great fatality, imagining all

you look upon. Lady, let me come in
to the other side where no one but your creator

has read your soul as I've dared,
hungry to be at one with you, your body.

I have loved you for your lovers' lies to you
inspired by yours, which they believed or not,

Léon swept up, Rodolphe believing he was faking it,
self-deceived both. Speak one word, Lady,

that I may enter your text, immortal.
One word would make us lovers in this life

before you climb back into your tomb, your book.
Before I return to my wife.

NOVEMBER: ANOTHER POEM ON MY BIRTHDAY

In the sky beyond this one, beyond imagining,
the trees look down on their mortal cousins.
Here, the panoply of turning is minute:
the copper beech, the maples various
like the birches, just as nature has reduced them,
one smear now, mashed across the ground.
More than half my life has passed by me
beneath that stare: there is so little time
to mulch and prune and strip the falling bark
even now, which my trees know, deciduous,
breaking, occupied with multifoliate causes
of disease. Just as my father, eighty-five,
called me at dawn, believing, I guess,
I should be up already, to wish me Happy Birthday.
Fifty-four, so young! so young! he said, but counting with me now.

THE CROW

All afternoon while the light falls
I have been fixing his grip for winter
on an apple tree at the center
of these trees dissolving in blue, on the dead one.

Now he is positioned, I let him
bring on the evening, accepting it.
I count out: in a minute he will be
extinguished, black feathers one with the night.

Lord, if you are here,
in my seasonal rite preparing
a god who sees me through until spring,
who is secret, between us, what are you?
You who must appear in darkness
or never, or nothing, or whatever I make up
from the wind? Only I? Only me?

DRIVING, CHRISTMAS EVE

past the Salvation Army Rehabilitation Center
I watch the plastic figures of the pastel crèche
assume their familiar positions on the wind
that loosened them at dusk again. Now this Mary, Joseph,
and the savior or imposter can be lit by a spotlight
Advent guarantees them one more time.

Now the grace I pray for, pulling to a stop
four years from the millennium
will appear or not. Oh, Child, I ask too much
when I believe in you and cannot make myself
stop my believing, even when the cracks deepen
in the cheap stand that, wobbling, holds you up.

Now wind shakes my car, shakes a lonely soul
loose from the Center, slamming across my hood
to stare straight up at me,
a knife snapping open in his hand.
Saw-toothed, his grin sways toward me, opening,
Find the child in me, the mouth would ask but can't.

So, the night is reborn after all, like this.
I stopped to entertain myself with the passing strange,
before heading home to my wife and children.
As if they can know: any move may be my last,
here, my life in my hands
with any motion of the wheel, any misspoken word
and my life can be checked in the balance on the scale of grace.
My life is in someone else's hands.

PSALM BEFORE SLEEP

Except for my body, who accompanies me
into this little death? Except for the stars
opening now on the vault overhead,

except for the barque I fit into so snugly,
my arms, my legs, shivering to dissolve,
dividing the great tides bearing me on.

Except for this song, the wind in my ears
which has joined the sky, reciting a black music
the constellations go on repeating in silence.

This is the way out: tomorrow I am someone else
I will meet face to face, the other shore arising.
This is the poem my words never bring back.

INCANTATION

I am in prayer! I tell myself tonight,
my body returning me from my fall
through windows in myself I never saw
a way out of until this minute.
And now I'm back and still alive.
I wish I could tell you the Christmas music
carried me on wings a few seconds back
looping through Day-Glow wreathes and Santa Claus
who appeared every few feet above the door of each shop,
a tiny god the shoppers looked up to as they passed.
I wish I could tell you I was only trembling
because it was Christmas Eve, when I would be received
by my wife and children in an hour, protected,
and be at home in myself with them
whose warming breath would take me in.
This would, yes, come to pass, but for the moment
which is this poem I am only grateful
the star had come and stood, cocked above my head
and passed me over: a salesclerk with a 38
had opened fire on children queuing up
to whisper last minute wishes in St. Nick's ear.
They are all dead; their little bodies like game birds
all six spread out, then carted off by three janitors
now scrubbing down the blood-streaked floor.
Who am I praying for, the dead or me or passersby
who have no reason to be among the living
any more than you, reader, or the man, handcuffed, gagged
who may be loose within a year to surprise one of us
but not me, we think, mumbling the old words
as I did, beginning this, words catching on the tongue
and if we're lucky, invoking someone.

FOR GREGOR SAMSA

Suppose you are the image of my risen body,
this carapace bearing its stiff brown wound

the apple, thrown, lodged in? Suppose the heaven
I can look forward to, my next life,

is nothing but your bedroom, the window we never flee,
in which I wake, endure, and come to die?

That there is a second death to hope for
if my first transform me into the very soul

I hid away, murderous, my almost every breath
I choked on, smiling, till soul became my flesh—

this is the solace for the monstrously grotesque
promise of eternal punishment. Gregor,

you offer hope: the charwoman bears you off,
your body flat, dry, empty, secretly.

Nights when I drop off now I am not
terrified, as I will be soon, to ask

the other side of life: who am I to myself
this morning, waking? Now I am here, today,

the man I was. And may or may not be
the shape of my own soul my next waking.

VESPERS

Now it is evening, the light rushes to fall
on a day disappearing into elemental shades,
the reddest red, blue's blue, the yellow yellowing going down.
Today is the first day of spring, lengthening
toward that ripening where it can start decline
from the long day in which I count each minute out
until dark falls and, exhausted, I am satisfied.

Mine is the world seen by Confucius, Jesus,
St. Teresa, by Dickinson, alone in her room,
facing a pit she opened on the floor, word by word,
granting her darkness as she spoke its resting place.
How can I dare to be afraid tonight,
part as I am of this earth turning to dust,
each breath propelling me by its eternity of motion?
How do I dare? Because I am nothing here,
light gone entirely now, like all of them,
like even one, without it gone.

TO THE READER

Just as this day is given me
to squander, hold or perfect,
so to the old woman wandering the highway's edge
I keep my side of, driving top speed off to work
where the way ahead abuts on broken glass
in which certain mornings a face can be assembled
if I lean close enough so my breath touches earth
and the dead grass makes as if to rise
and she and I, when she is not too drunk,
cursing herself for falling there last night,
we see together the tracery of a saint's face
such as becomes those in Byzantine mosaics . . . .
How I would like to tell her as I tell you, reader,
that often I will become her in my next lives
as in the one just over I was her father
and wept that she was born to end like this,
driven past by a man bent on the day alone,
occupied with himself, pretending he could be one person.

EVENTIDES

As it has and will, the sea
continues tonight to suffer changes
in pitch, the direction of that music
flooding the rocks where we are sitting.
Minute by minute it is here and disappearing.
And the skyline where the last wave meets the night, descending,
this, too, is a melody, slower
in the fall toward darkness, a procession
suggesting the space there might be infinite.
How many years have we not found our differences,
raging before, appeased in resting here,
a man and a woman listening to such waters,
looking out at their expressionless one face.
If there is a world beyond this body
we will not be together in such ceremonies, I think,
but may happen to meet in chance companies.
No need to be reconciled then,
no need for anything, one wave beside another
morning, evening, leaving, coming in.

POEM ON THE FIRST DAY OF SPRING

Everyone should write a Spring poem—Louise Glück

Never, in the way of the Great Poets,
have I yearned to find myself in the domain of Nature,
rising, while first buds stud the trees,
to burst into a woman, open to the season.
Such anguish as it laid bare in them
I pity every famous ancient. Yes,
I despise their assumption: that we begin again in Spring.
Love, it is April, first light.
Listen, the birds, returned, pluck out ancient melodies.
Leave the shades drawn, let night stall in our bed.
Turn to me, naked, in no new way at all
but rolling our seasons into one, nameless.
How many years have we perfected this? Countless.
Losing track, each time is last, delicious, perilous.

INVITATION TO THE VOYAGE

Every body desires its own death.
Even my son in fever suffers this tonight
as I witness, all his eleven years
raging to escape, the tossing limbs
ablaze. So, too, my aunt
my last visit to the home informed me,
My time has come to go, why can't I?
and then voyaged as she spoke across the years
back to her sixth birthday and left my body
standing there, her eyes fixed
on some other me, one of her party guests:
Where did you put my present?
You who read this: I have to speak for you,
reader, don't I? You and I, staggering
through middle age together, why should I
confess my travels across the center line
dividing the highway, how I ride the left side
deliberately, just to keep in shape
that I may touch the edge of something sinister.
Reader, hypocrite, I want you to enter the poem tonight
that I can dismantle these lines, I want
the impossible, for you to speak!
Reader, my double, my brother, my sister,
come close down, over the page. Pray for me.

CARNEGIE MELLON POETRY

1975
The Living and the Dead, Ann Hayes
In the Face of Descent, T. Alan Broughton

1976
The Week the Dirigible Came, Jay Meek
Full of Lust and Good Usage, Stephen Dunn

1977
How I Escaped from the Labyrinth and Other Poems,
        Philip Dacey
The Lady from the Dark Green Hills, Jim Hall
For Luck: Poems 1962-1977, H.L. Van Brunt
By the Wreckmaster's Cottage, Paula Rankin

1978
New & Selected Poems, James Bertolino
The Sun Fetcher, Michael Dennis Browne
A Circus of Needs, Stephen Dunn
The Crowd Inside, Elizabeth Libbey

1979
Paying Back the Sea, Philip Dow
Swimmer in the Rain, Robert Wallace
Far from Home, T. Alan Broughton
The Room Where Summer Ends, Peter Cooley
No Ordinary World, Mekeel McBride

1980
And the Man Who Was Traveling Never Got Home,
        H.L. Van Brunt
Drawing on the Walls, Jay Meek
The Yellow House on the Corner, Rita Dove
The 8-Step Grapevine, Dara Wier
The Mating Reflex, Jim Hall

1981
A Little Faith, John Skoyles
Augers, Paula Rankin
Walking Home from the Icehouse, Vern Rutsala
Work and Love, Stephen Dunn
The Rote Walker, Mark Jarman
Morocco Journal, Richard Harteis
Songs of a Returning Soul, Elizabeth Libbey

1982
The Granary, Kim R. Stafford
Calling the Dead, C.G. Hanzlicek
Dreams Before Sleep, T. Alan Broughton
Sorting It Out, Anne S. Perlman
Love Is Not a Consolation; It Is a Light, Primus St. John

1983
The Going Under of the Evening Land, Mekeel McBride
Museum, Rita Dove
Air and Salt, Eve Shelnutt
Nightseasons, Peter Cooley

1984
Falling from Stardom, Jonathan Holden
Miracle Mile, Ed Ochester
Girlfriends and Wives, Robert Wallace
Earthly Purposes, Jay Meek
Not Dancing, Stephen Dunn
The Man in the Middle, Gregory Djanikian
A Heart Out of This World, David James
All You Have in Common, Dara Wier

1985
Smoke from the Fires, Michael Dennis Browne
Full of Lust and Good Usage, Stephen Dunn *(2nd edition)*
Far and Away, Mark Jarman
Anniversary of the Air, Michael Waters
To the House Ghost, Paula Rankin
Midwinter Transport, Anne Bromley

1986
Seals in the Inner Harbor, Brendan Galvin
Thomas and Beulah, Rita Dove
Further Adventures With You, C.D. Wright
Fifteen to Infinity, Ruth Fainlight
False Statements, Jim Hall
When There Are No Secrets, C.G. Hanzlicek

1987
Some Gangster Pain, Gillian Conoley
Other Children, Lawrence Raab
Internal Geography, Richard Harteis
The Van Gogh Notebook, Peter Cooley
A Circus of Needs, Stephen Dunn (2nd edition)
Ruined Cities, Vern Rutsala
Places and Stories, Kim R. Stafford

1988
Preparing to Be Happy, T. Alan Broughton
Red Letter Days, Mekeel McBride
The Abandoned Country, Thomas Rabbitt
The Book of Knowledge, Dara Wier
Changing the Name to Ochester, Ed Ochester
Weaving the Sheets, Judith Root

1989
Recital in a Private Home, Eve Shelnutt
A Walled Garden, Michael Cuddihy
The Age of Krypton, Carol J. Pierman
Land That Wasn't Ours, David Keller
Stations, Jay Meek
The Common Summer: New and Selected Poems, Robert Wallace
The Burden Lifters, Michael Waters
Falling Deeply into America, Gregory Djanikian
Entry in an Unknown Hand, Franz Wright

1990
Why the River Disappears, Marcia Southwick
Staying Up For Love, Leslie Adrienne Miller
Dreamer, Primus St. John

1991
Permanent Change, John Skoyles
Clackamas, Gary Gildner
Tall Stranger, Gillian Conoley
The Gathering of My Name, Cornelius Eady
A Dog in the Lifeboat, Joyce Peseroff
Raised Underground, Renate Wood
Divorce: A Romance, Paula Rankin

1992
Modern Ocean, James Harms
The Astonished Hours, Peter Cooley
You Won't Remember This, Michael Dennis Browne
Twenty Colors, Elizabeth Kirschner
First A Long Hesitation, Eve Shelnutt
Bountiful, Michael Waters
Blue for the Plough, Dara Wier
All That Heat in a Cold Sky, Elizabeth Libbey

1993
Trumpeter, Jeannine Savard
Cuba, Ricardo Pau-Llosa
The Night World and the Word Night, Franz Wright
The Book of Complaints, Richard Katrovas

1994
If Winter Come: Collected Poems, 1967–1992, Alvin Aubert
Of Desire and Disorder, Wayne Dodd
Ungodliness, Leslie Adrienne Miller
Rain, Henry Carlile
Windows, Jay Meek
A Handful of Bees, Dzvinia Orlowsky

1995
Germany, Caroline Finkelstein
Housekeeping in a Dream, Laura Kasischke
About Distance, Gregory Djanikian
Wind of the White Dresses, Mekeel McBride
Above the Tree Line, Kathy Mangan
In the Country of Elegies, T. Alan Broughton
Scenes from the Light Years, Anne C. Bromley
Quartet, Angela Ball

1996
Back Roads, Patricia Henley
Dyer's Thistle, Peter Balakian
Beckon, Gillian Conoley
The Parable of Fire, James Reiss
Cold Pluto, Mary Ruefle
Orders of Affection, Arthur Smith
Colander, Michael McFee

1997
Growing Darkness, Growing Light, Jean Valentine
Selected Poems, 1965-1995, Michael Dennis Browne
Your Rightful Childhood: New and Selected Poems, Paula Rankin
Headlands: New and Selected Poems, Jay Meek
Soul Train, Allison Joseph
The Autobiography of a Jukebox, Cornelius Eady
The Patience of the Cloud Photographer, Elizabeth Holmes
Madly in Love, Aliki Barnstone
An Octave Above Thunder: New and Selected Poems, Carol Muske

1998
Yesterday Had a Man in It, Leslie Adrienne Miller
Definition of the Soul, John Skoyles
Dithyrambs, Richard Katrovas
Postal Routes, Elizabeth Kirschner
The Blue Salvages, Wayne Dodd
The Joy Addict, James Harms
Clemency, Colette Inez
Scattering the Ashes, Jeff Friedman
Sacred Conversations, Peter Cooley
Life Among the Trolls, Maura Stanton